South Carolina

BY HOLLY SAARI

Published by The Child's World®
1980 Lookout Drive • Mankato, MN 56003-1705
800-599-READ • www.childsworld.com

ACKNOWLEDGMENTS
The Child's World®: Mary Berendes, Publishing Director
The Design Lab: Design and production
Red Line Editorial: Editorial direction

PHOTO CREDITS: Stacie Stauff Smith Photography/Shutterstock Images, cover,
1, 3; Matt Kania/Map Hero, Inc., 4, 5; Denis Jr. Tangney/iStockphoto, 7, 21;
John Upchurch/iStockphoto, 9; iStockphoto, 10; David Walker/iStockphoto, 11;
Lynn Eodice/Photolibrary, 13; North Wind Picture Archives/Photolibrary, 15;
James C. Pruitt/iStockphoto, 17; Michael Dwyer/AP Images, 19; One Mile Up,
22; Quarter-dollar coin image from the United States Mint, 22

LIBRARY OF CONGRESS CATALOGING-IN-PUBLICATION DATA
Saari, Holly.
  South Carolina / by Holly Saari.
      p. cm.
  Includes bibliographical references and index.
  ISBN 978-1-60253-485-8 (library bound : alk. paper)
  1. South Carolina—Juvenile literature. I. Title.

F269.3.S23 2010
975.7—dc22

                                    2010019325

Printed in the United States of America in Mankato, Minnesota.
July 2010
F11538

On the cover:
Many people
enjoy South
Carolina's
beaches and
warm weather.

CONTENTS

Geography

Let's explore South Carolina! South Carolina is in the southeastern part of the United States. It is next to the Atlantic Ocean.

NORTH CAROLINA

Spartanburg •

Rock Hill •

Greenville •

NORTH
WEST · EAST
SOUTH

Greenwood •

• Florence

★ Columbia

SOUTH CAROLINA

Myrtle Beach •

Aiken •

Georgetown •

GEORGIA

Charleston •

Beaufort •

Atlantic
Ocean

Hilton Head Island

Cities

Columbia is the capital of South Carolina. It is the largest city in the state. Charleston is a well-known city. These cities have many large, historic houses. They also have art **museums**.

About 120,000 people live in Columbia. ▶

Land

The land next to the Atlantic Ocean is flat. The middle of the state is hilly. The northwest has mountains. The state has many **swamps**. It also has several rivers.

Table Rock State Park in the northern part of South Carolina has hills and mountains. ▶

9

Plants and Animals

South Carolina has 46 state parks. The state tree is the palmetto tree. It has green **palms**, which are large leaves. The state bird is the Carolina wren. Many people in the state have flower gardens. The state flower is the yellow jessamine.

Palmetto logs were used to build important South Carolina forts. ▶

People and Work

About 4.5 million people live in South Carolina. Some people work in health care and **tourism**. **Manufacturing** is important in the state. Workers make items such as clothes, paper products, and **chemicals**. Some people work on farms. Farmers in South Carolina raise chickens and cattle.

Some important South Carolina crops are tobacco, corn, cotton, and peaches.

Some tourism workers give tours of Charleston. ▶

History

People from Europe began to settle in the area that is now South Carolina in the 1500s. About 30 Native American **tribes** already lived there. More European settlements began in the 1600s. South Carolina became the eighth state on May 23, 1788.

Early settlers prepared the land for farming. ▶

Ways of Life

South Carolina has many museums. They show art, items from wars and battles, and the state's history. Many people also visit the state's beaches. South Carolina's many golf courses are **popular**, too.

A family enjoys a South Carolina beach. ▶

Famous People

Jesse Jackson is a **civil rights** leader who was born in South Carolina. Boxer Joe Frazier was born in South Carolina, too. "Shoeless" Joe Jackson was a famous baseball player from South Carolina. Basketball player Kevin Garnett was also born in the state.

Kevin Garnett helped the Boston Celtics win the NBA Championship in 2008. ▶

Famous Places

Many battles of the **American Revolution** were fought in South Carolina. Visitors can see people act out some of these battles. The first shot of the U.S. **Civil War** was fired at Fort Sumter in South Carolina.

Myrtle Beach is a popular vacation spot. The beach is 60 miles (97 km) long.

Many colorful homes and buildings line the coast in Myrtle Beach. ▶

State Symbols

Seal

South Carolina's seal has a palmetto tree. It also shows a goddess walking on a beach. Go to childsworld.com/links for a link to South Carolina's state Web site, where you can get a firsthand look at the state seal.

Flag

South Carolina's flag has a white palmetto tree and a white **crescent** moon.

Quarter

The South Carolina state quarter shows the state tree, bird, and flower. The quarter came out in 2000.

Glossary

American Revolution (uh-MER-ih-kin rev-uh-LOO-shun): During the American Revolution, from 1775 to 1783, the 13 American colonies fought against Britain for their independence. Many battles of the American Revolution were fought in South Carolina.

chemicals (KEM-uh-kulz): Chemicals are substances used in chemistry. Chemicals are made in South Carolina.

civil rights (SIV-il RITES): Civil rights are the rights every human should have. Jesse Jackson is a civil rights leader from South Carolina.

Civil War (SIV-il WOR): In the United States, the Civil War was a war fought between the Northern and the Southern states from 1861 to 1865. Many Civil War battles were fought in South Carolina.

crescent (KRESS-unt): Crescent means something is shaped like the moon when it is skinny. A crescent moon is on the South Carolina state flag.

manufacturing (man-yuh-FAK-chur-ing): Manufacturing is the task of making items with machines. Many people work in manufacturing jobs in South Carolina.

museums (myoo-ZEE-umz): Museums are places where people go to see art, history, or science displays. Visitors to South Carolina can see museums.

palms (PAHLMZ): Palms are large, green, tropical trees; palms can also refer to the fan-like leaves of a palm tree. South Carolina's state tree has green palms.

popular (POP-yuh-lur): To be popular is to be enjoyed by many people. Myrtle Beach is a popular place in South Carolina.

seal (SEEL): A seal is a symbol a state uses for government business. South Carolina's state seal has a palmetto tree.

swamps (SWAHMPS): Swamps are areas of land that have plants and are covered in water. South Carolina has swamps.

symbols (SIM-bulz): Symbols are pictures or things that stand for something else. The seal and the flag are South Carolina's symbols.

tourism (TOOR-ih-zum): Tourism is visiting another place (such as a state or country) for fun or the jobs that help these visitors. Tourism is popular in South Carolina.

tribes (TRYBZ): Tribes are groups of people who share ancestors and customs. Native American tribes lived in the South Carolina area when settlers from Europe first came.

Further Information

Books

Keller, Laurie. *The Scrambled States of America*. New York: Henry Holt, 2002.

Martonyi, E. Andrew. *The Little Man In the Map: With Clues To Remember All 50 States*. Woodland Hills, CA: Schoolside Press, 2007.

Thornton, Brian. *The Everything Kids' States Book: Wind Your Way Across Our Great Nation*. Avon, MA: Adams Media, 2007.

Web Sites

Visit our Web site for links about South Carolina: *childsworld.com/links*

Note to Parents, Teachers, and Librarians: We routinely verify our Web links to make sure they are safe and active sites. So encourage your readers to check them out!

Index